Stan Lee

Comic Book Writer & Creator of *Spider-Man*

by Grace Hansen

Abdo

HISTORY MAKER BIOGRAPHIES

Kids

abdopublishing.com

Published by Abdo Kids, a division of ABDO, P.O. Box 398166, Minneapolis, Minnesota 55439.
Copyright © 2018 by Abdo Consulting Group, Inc. International copyrights reserved in all countries.
No part of this book may be reproduced in any form without written permission from the publisher.
Abdo Kids Jumbo™ is a trademark and logo of Abdo Kids.

Printed in the United States of America, North Mankato, Minnesota.

102017

012018

Photo Credits: Alamy, AP Images, Getty Images, iStock, Seth Poppel/Yearbook Library, Shutterstock,
©Pop Culture Geek p.7 / CC-SA-BY 2.0

Production Contributors: Teddy Borth, Jennie Forsberg, Grace Hansen

Design Contributors: Dorothy Toth, Laura Mitchell

Publisher's Cataloging in Publication Data

Names: Hansen, Grace, author.

Title: Stan Lee: comic-book writer & creator of Spider-Man / by Grace Hansen.

Other titles: Comic-book writer & creator of Spider-Man | Comic-book writer and creator of Spider-Man

Description: Minneapolis, Minnesota : Abdo Kids, 2018. | Series: History maker biographies |
    Includes glossary, index and online resource (page 24).

Identifiers: LCCN 2017943568 | ISBN 9781532104305 (lib.bdg.) | ISBN 9781532105425 (ebook) |
    ISBN 9781532105982 (Read-to-me ebook)

Subjects: LCSH: Lee, Stan--1922- --Juvenile literature. | Cartoonists--United States--Biography--Juvenile
    literature. | Marvel Comics--Juvenile literature.

Classification: DDC 741.5092 [B]--dc23

LC record available at https://lccn.loc.gov/2017943568

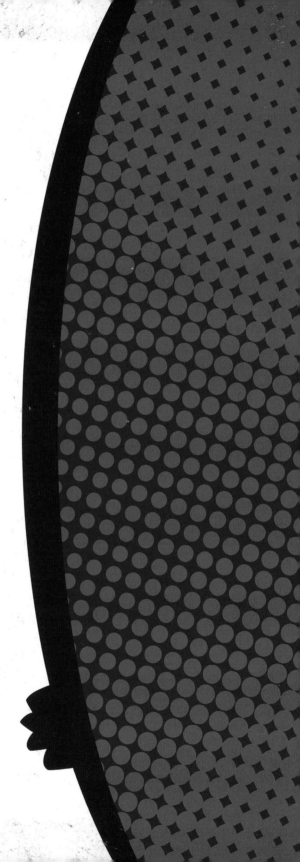

Table of Contents

Early Years

Stanley Martin Lieber was born on December 28, 1922. He grew up in New York City. His parents were Romanian **immigrants**.

New York

Stan loved books and movies as a child. He worked odd jobs in high school. In 1939, he got a job as an assistant at Timely Publications.

Lieber to Lee

Stan also worked as an editor at the company. He shortened his name from Lieber to Lee. Later, Timely changed its name to Marvel.

Marvel had to compete with DC Comics. Lee's boss asked him to create a team of superheroes.

11

Fantastic Four and More

Lee wrote the Fantastic Four in 1961. His superheroes were not perfect. They had human **faults**. Fans related to them.

13

Lee created more Marvel characters soon after. Some popular ones include the Hulk and Spider-Man.

Hollywood!

Lee took on more responsibility at Marvel. In 1981, Lee and his family moved to California. He wanted to be involved in Marvel's film **ventures**.

Many of Lee's superheroes became blockbusters. The popular *Spider-Man* was released in 2002. In 2008, Robert Downey Jr. starred in *Iron Man*.

The Avengers and *Captain America: Civil War* are two of Marvel's biggest hits. Stan Lee's characters are loved by many. He changed the comic book world!

Timeline

Leiber gets a job as an office assistant at Timely Publications.

Timely changes its name to *Marvel Comics*. Lee creates *The Fantastic Four* to compete with DC's *Justice League of America*.

Lee creates *The Amazing Spider-Man*.

***The Avengers* the movie debuts in theaters.**

1939

1961

1963

2012

1922

1941

1962

1981

December 28
Stanley Martin Leiber is born in New York City.

Lee is promoted to editor at Timely Comics.

Lee creates *The Incredible Hulk*.

Lee and his family move to California.

Glossary

blockbuster – a film that is very successful and often has a very high budget.

editor – a person who reads and corrects materials for publication.

fault – a moral weakness or imperfection.

immigrant – a person who moves permanently to another country from his or her native land.

venture – to start to do something new or different that sometimes involves risk.

Index

Abdo Kids
ONLINE
FREE! ONLINE MULTIMEDIA RESOURCES

Visit **abdokids.com** and use this code to access crafts, games, videos, and more!

Abdo Kids Code:
HSK4305

24